My Blue

Judaic Traditions in Literature, Music, and Art
Harold Bloom and Ken Frieden, *Series Editors*

Other titles in Judaic Traditions in Literature, Music, and Art

Early Yiddish Epic
Jerold C. Frakes, ed. and trans.

Letters to America: Selected Poems of Reuven Ben-Yosef
Michael Weingrad, ed. and trans.

My Friendship with Martin Buber
Maurice Friedman

Rhetoric and Nation: The Formation of Hebrew National Culture, 1880–1990
Shai P. Ginsburg

Social Concern and Left Politics in Jewish American Art: 1880–1940
Matthew Baigell

The Travels of Benjamin Zuskin
Ala Zuskin Perelman

Who Will Die Last: Stories of Life in Israel
David Ehrlich; Ken Frieden, ed.

Yiddish Poetry and the Tuberculosis Sanatorium: 1900–1970
Ernest B. Gilman

My Blue Piano

Else Lasker-Schüler

Poems Translated from the German by

Brooks Haxton

BILINGUAL EDITION

Syracuse University Press

First Edition 2015
15 16 17 18 19 20 6 5 4 3 2 1

∞ The paper used in this publication meets the minimum requirements of the American National Standard for Information Sciences—Permanence of Paper for Printed Library Materials, ANSI Z39.48-1992.

For a listing of books published and distributed by Syracuse University Press, visit www.SyracuseUniversityPress.syr.edu.

ISBN: 978-0-8156-3420-1 (cloth) 978-0-8156-1056-4 (paperback)
978-0-8156-5336-3 (e-book)

Library of Congress Cataloging-in-Publication Data

Available from the publisher upon request.

Manufactured in the United States of America

These translations are dedicated
to the memory of my grandmother,
Ellise Blum Haxton

Contents

Note on the Selection of Poems

The translator made this selection to introduce readers of English to a variety of Else Lasker-Schüler's poetry at its best. The order of the poems here is largely chronological, starting with the first collection from Berlin in 1902 and ending with the last, from Jerusalem in 1943. The date of the first collection to include each poem appears under the German text of the poem. Two poems which the poet published in more than one book have been placed among the poems of the later work, but the date given is that of the earlier collection in which the poems appeared.

Introduction

Despite Victorian mores, many of Freud's contemporaries knew from having studied Greek in school that Eros rules all other gods and mortals, according to Hesiod, "over-powering the intelligence in the breast." With his sexual theory, Freud helped bring back that early sense of Eros, which had undergone strange transformations even in the Classical age. Plato in his *Symposium*, and some of the vase painters in the centuries before Plato, venerated Eros as the eldest of the gods. Later Eros appeared as a man in his prime, fully bearded, then as a beardless youth, and, later still, as a boy. By the time of the Romans, he had begun to be seen as a baby with bow and arrow, his wings, once emblems of an awe-inspiring power from the cosmic egg, now mere comic decoration.

Freud's Eros is not the infant Cupid of erotic comedy, but the older god revered by philosophers and poets. Robert Graves has written that this god, known in Orphic rites as Phanes or Revealer, was the first deific power to emerge from Chaos: Orphic Eros, according to the sources cited by Graves, was not a person but a force, which "set the universe in motion" and "created earth, sky, sun, and moon." Said by some to be the sun itself, the Revealer was also a monstrous beast, "double-sexed and golden-winged . . . having four heads," a creature who "sometimes roared like a bull or a lion, sometimes hissed like a serpent or bleated like a ram."[1]

When the idea of poet as passionate Romantic was beginning to spread through Europe, Hölderlin and others revived the unruly spirit of the Orphic hymns. In 1830, audiences rioted at Victor Hugo's *Hernani*, a play about a noblewoman's forbidden love for a bandit. The novelist George Sand left her husband the baron that same year, and settled in the disreputable Paris of bohemians, where her young lovers, she let everybody know, included two geniuses of Romantic poetry and music, Musset and Chopin. Forty years later, the erotic display of art and artist was no less the rage. Sarah Bernhardt, the most respected actor and the most notorious woman in the world, starred in new productions of the plays of Hugo, Sand, Musset, and others, while conducting flagrant sexual affairs with a number of the most renowned writers, actors, artists, and political figures of her time, both men and women.

In 1869, when Bernhardt was cross-dressing, à la George Sand, for her first great critical success, the lead as troubadour in Coppée's *Le Passant*, Elisabeth Schüler was born near Düsseldorf, into a Jewish banking family. After providing for their daughter's pampered, dreamy childhood, both her parents died when she was in her twenties, and her lukewarm marriage to a physician, Dr. Berthold Lasker, failed. From the second of the bourgeois households that had been her life, the

1. Robert Graves, *The Greek Myths* (London: Penguin Books, 1955), 1:30.

fledgling poet stepped into the streets of Berlin, the hotbed of early Expressionism.

Now, at thirty, having just become the mother of a son she said was illegitimate, she lived, for the first time, from hand to mouth, in temporary lodgings, as she would for more than forty years until she died. In the early poem "Chaos," she evokes Eros as the Orphic power at the threshold of being, source of infant vitality, nurturing maternal love, sexual ecstasy, and suffering:

> If only hurt could stir,
> I wish, and plunge me
> into a suffering self,
> for a god of pleasure
> to ferry me home
> under my mother's breast!
>
> My motherland is soulless.
> No rose blooms
> on the tepid air. —
> . . . . But o that my heart's most tender love
> could bury me in his flesh.

She often dramatized herself as a Romantic figure. But like Whitman, who remade himself in his thirties with similar erotic brio, she appeared to most of her contemporaries simply odd. Her social standing, as a Jew and a disreputable woman, seems to have drawn her to identify with ancient peoples from Tibet, Persia, and Egypt more than with her fellow Germans. In "Homesick," one of her best-known poems, she represents her personal alienation by playing the changes on the story of exile familiar from the tradition of the Passover celebration:

The speech of this
cold country is not mine.
Nor can I keep the pace.

Even the clouds
escape me.

Night here is a foisted queen.

And still I bear in mind
wild places pharaohs ride.
I kiss the likeness
of Egyptian stars.

My lips shine
from outlandishness,

and I am the picturebook
glistening in your lap.

But tears weave silk
threads down your face.

My opalescent birds
with enlaid coral gouged away

in garden hedges feel
their soft nests turning into stone.

And those who anointed the palace of my dead,
they carried the crowns of my fathers,
prayers they sang at the holy river sank.

Influenced, no doubt, by the public personae of George Sand and Sarah Bernhardt, Else Lasker-Schüler often dressed in theatrical costume as a Persian girl or an Egyptian boy.

On the stage of cafe nightlife in Berlin, she created for herself the role of poet as notorious woman. The boldness of this undertaking for a Jew in Germany, where the only two women widely known as poets had been noblewomen and Christian devotionalists, would be difficult to exaggerate.

One best-selling book in Paris at the turn of the century was *Les Femmes d'Isräel*, an anti-Semitic, anti-feminist tract written in the midst of the Dreyfus affair. The book devotes its whole last chapter to deriding Bernhardt as the epitome of the Jewish libertine. Commenting on Bernhardt's status as the daughter of a Jewish mother who sent her to be educated in Catholic schools, the authors say: "Whether initiated into the worship of God by Gemara or by catechism, Sarah Bernhardt is neither more nor less than a Jewess and nothing but a Jewess."[2]

Lasker-Schüler, despite this widespread wish to typify and isolate Jews, was steadfastly cosmopolitan. She wrote devotional poems as midrash on Hebrew scripture and as Christian hymns, though she was not devout in her Judaism nor a convert to Christianity. Her poem about the Virgin Mary bears an interesting relation to poems by Rilke, today her most celebrated contemporary, although then less critically acclaimed than she. Rilke was, like her, a student of religions, including ancient cults and Islam, though he was sometimes candid in his anti-Semitism, remarking, for example, that Franz Werfel's personal presence, as a "Jewboy," interfered with one's sense

2. Francois Bournand and Raphael Viau, *Les Femmes d'Israël* (Paris: Librairie A. Pierret, 1898), 221. As cited in Janis Bergman-Carton, "Negotiating the Categories: Sarah Bernhardt and the Possibility of Jewishness," *Art Journal* 55, no. 2 (1996): 55.

of the "purity" in his verse.[3] Rilke called his own series of poems on the life of Mary "*Das Marienleben*," a traditional name for church panels depicting such scenes. Lasker-Schüler's "Mary of Nazareth" also recalls traditions in religious painting, unsurprisingly, since both Rilke and Lasker-Schüler had immersed themselves in the culture of the visual artists who were their friends:

> Dreamer, dawdler, young maid Mary,
> everywhere a wind from the roses
> quenching the black, black stars —
> cradle in your arms that peeping soul.
>
> All the children are coming
> on lambs, toddler on toddler
> to see the godling.
>
> Hedges overflow
> with blossom,
> and all that vastness wrapped
> in a little blue shirt.

Apropos of the lilting rhythm, consonance, and assonance in this translation, I have tried, where rhyme and meter give the German something of the lilt of ballad or song lyric, to

3. Ralph Freedman. *Life of a Poet: Rainer Maria Rilke.* (New York: Farrar, Straus and Giroux, 1996), 370. Freedman quotes the reference to Werfel from Rilke's letter to Princess Marie von Thurn und Taxis. One reviewer points out that the notes in Freedman's book indicate that Rilke also wrote the same comment to his Jewish friend and patron, the poet Hugo von Hoffmamnsthal: Lee Siegel, "To Work Is to Live Without Dying," *The Atlantic Monthly* 277, no. 4 (April 1996): 112–118.

bring my English close to the cadence and flavor of the originals. For some of the earlier poems I find that imitating the pattern of end rhyme helps to generate a similar tone. For unrhymed poems, like this one, and for the rhymed poems written after Lasker-Schüler turned toward free-verse couplets as her usual format, an underlying metricality, with assonance and consonance inside the line, suggest to my ear an effect more like that in the German.

As for literal accuracy, while I am on the subject of translation, I mean to give a speaking likeness of the original. In some poems I have come closer to the literal sense of the German than previous translators. Elsewhere, I take liberties in the belief that a freer version sometimes can deliver more fidelity to the effect than doggedly accurate paraphrase. My approach to the balance between literal accuracy and poetic effect has been unprogrammatic.

Lasker-Schüler's poems have been praised by critics in her own country as the work of a German Sappho, and celebrated by such various and eminent fellow poets as Georg Trakl, Gottfried Benn, and Yehuda Amichai (the Hebrew poet having been a native speaker of German). Others have deplored her work as immature and overwritten. In English, Blake and Dickinson have drawn similar reproach from conventional critics whose taste in retrospect seems narrow. I leave arguments about Lasker-Schüler's eccentric German style to native speakers of her language. Disagreements about style, character, and taste seem likely to persist among her readers, as they have for centuries in the discussion of poems by Sir Thomas Wyatt, though most readers with an interest in the history of English writing now find Wyatt's style remarkably vigorous. Not coincidentally, the erotic declarations of Wyatt, Blake,

Whitman, and Dickinson, as well as those of other experimenters in English poetry, including Shakespeare, have also excited controversy.

Auden, troubled by esthetic and imaginative narrowness, once wrote that critics who deny Shakespeare his homoeroticism clearly find it difficult to permit their bard experiences they cannot imagine as a possibility for themselves. Auden thought that the cultivation of taste should yield a broader and broader range of experiences, each more deeply distinctive. In the expansive spirit of Auden's thinking, I have tried to give readers of English something of the distinct flavor of these poems.

Soon after Lasker-Schüler helped create the role of poet as fiery woman and subverter of the status quo, Anna Akhmatova began to publish and to make appearances at the Stray Dog Cabaret in St. Petersburg. When Akhmatova's father felt that her writing was a blot on the family name of Gorenko, she took the Tatar surname of her grandmother, feeling that its ethnic flavor fit the daring spirit of her work. Notorious women from several countries soon made names as poets, among them, from the United States, Sara Teasdale, Elinor Wylie, H. D., and Edna St. Vincent Millay.

While Sarah Bernhardt in her sixties still earned praise for playing young romantic leads of either gender, Lasker-Schüler in her middle age appeared in costume, often as a boy, reciting in an "Arabian tongue" of her own invention and claiming to be as much as thirty years younger than she unmistakably was. However silly she may have appeared in her extravagant trappings, she seems in hindsight that much more heroic: dreaming up, against the dominant patterns of German culture, flagrant counter-dramas, featuring herself in the role of radically free woman and androgynous Jew in Arab clothing, her passion for the imagination and for her people enriched with flourishes of Persia, Egypt, and Tibet, together with a dash of Christian lore.

Sensual ecstasy as a religious experience pervades her work from beginning to end. Her fervor can be almost wholly sexual, as in "Fortissimo," where she imagines herself and her lover falling to the Turkish carpet in a fit of lovemaking, "gone wild and screaming like gazelles." "My Lovesong," like many of her poems, describes erotic attraction as a kind of physical and spiritual state of possession, in Hesiod's phrase, "overpowering the intelligence in the breast":

Wellings homeborn in my blood
murmur me always, always you.

Under the staggering moon
my naked dreams go dancing, searching,
children who sleepwalk softly
beyond the gloom of the hedgerows.

O, but your lips, your sunwarm
drunken scented lips . . . all day
from clustered silver-blue-streaked flowers,
you, your lips, you smiling, you.

And always the snakelike rippling
of gooseflesh
over my shoulder down . . .
I listen . . .

Wellings homeborn in my blood
murmur me always, always . . .

She wrote with equal intensity about lovers, friendships, family, social causes, and religion. She was rhapsodic, for example, in her praise of the Catholic social worker, Karl Sonnenschein, and in her elegies for the social activist Johannes Holzmann, a beloved friend whom she visited while he was dying in an imperial Russian prison, after he had been driven out of Germany for his advocacy of social justice and sexual liberation. Holzmann was particularly outspoken about the oppression of homosexuals, though he seems to have been, like Lasker-Schüler, heterosexual, and several sources refer to them as lovers, an assertion which other sources refute. The name she gave him, "Senna Hoy," which is the title of this poem, reverses the letters of his first name.

With you lying under the hill
the earth is sweet.

When I go near on tiptoe,
I walk the holiest paths.

Softly the roses of your blood leave
death drenched through and through.

Now I have no fear
of dying.

On your grave I burst
into bloom like a briar.

Your lips have called me always,
and now my name finds no way back.

Every shovelful of earth between us
buries me also.

Night, therefore, is always mine,
and stars already in the dusk.

And I am fathomless to our friends
and am become a stranger.

But you stand at the city gate in the hush
awaiting me, my tall angel.

In most of her poetry, as in the Orphic hymns, the Song of Songs, Sufi love poems, and in other parallel traditions, the erotic is a permutation of the sacred. She expresses the turbulent psychology of a fundamentally ecstatic relation to being, the supernatural charge ignited by earthliness.

The play of power in these dramas is as troubling as we might expect. In "Dream" the speaker dreams of being raped as the fulfillment of a demonic attraction. In "Answer" she calmly considers her power to hurt the lover toward whom her feelings have cooled. In "Pharaoh and Joseph," Joseph speaks of himself as he appears in the dreams of Pharaoh, who has rejected the royal wives for the comfort of his minister's sexual embrace.

Often, as in her poem "To the Golden Knight," the one who speaks can feel already, even in the moment of ecstasy, the loss implicit in such passion:

All there is of gold
in this great world is you.

For you I search the stars
and have no wish to sleep.

We two shall lie down by the hedgerow
never to rise up again.

Let's kiss the sweet stuff
of this daydream from each other's hands.

My heart plucks
roses at your mouth.

From this eye into you love skips;
you track its butterflies.

What shall I do now
when you go.

Black snow
trickles from my lids;

when I am dead,
play this way with my soul.

When hearts personified pluck roses, and butterflies skip from one lover's eye into another's, as they do here, intellectuals often recoil from what they label kitsch. Angels, children, forest creatures, moonlight, and heavenly love appear in Lasker-Schüler's poems again and again. A serious writer learns, the experts tell us, to pare away these rank vulgarities. But the *dread* of kitsch is a convention that deserves our scrutiny as well. Ironic distance, in fact, is no more intelligent than the expression of feeling; coolness is not authenticity; and critical dogma is weak as a response to tenderness. Poetry, Lasker-Schüler reminds us, can help people find their way beyond conventional shame into the lost possibility of emotional life. The imaginative challenge of this renewal may involve, for some of us, the deliberate cultivation of taste described by Auden.

As for stock phrases, images, and scenes, scholars have taught us, in reading from medieval ballads and sonnets of the Renaissance, and from the earlier Greek, Mandarin, and Sanskrit, to experience repeated threads in the cultural fabric not as howlers but as markers of depth. When the conventions of print displace those of song, contempt for what we call cliché is one result. But Lasker-Schüler, like Blake straitjacketed by the Enlightenment, deliberately flouts decorum, preferring to stray in topic, grammar, spelling, and diction. As a result, a British reviewer for The *Times Literary Supplement*, having identified Lasker-Schüler in 1921 as "one of the best-known living German writers," notes that he finds it "less and less easy to forget, in reading her work, that she is also a Jewess" whose "style has a kind of Oriental luxuriousness . . . which a purely German writer would not display."[4] It is difficult in translation to reproduce her stylistic singularities. But I hope these versions of her poems represent, in the expression of unguarded emotion, as in Blake's songs, besides exoticism, an affinity with traditions popular in ballad and hymn. The use of exotic and popular materials by a cosmopolitan artist often involves irony and satire. But anyone who doubts that Lasker-Schüler or Blake, Whitman or Lawrence passionately celebrated the mystery of Eros the Revealer, also known as Eleutherios, the Liberator, simply has not paid attention.

Lifelong receptivity toward the fringes of European culture made her and her second husband, the theorist and composer Georg Lewin, whom she renamed Herwath Walden, leaders of Expressionism. She also coined the name for her

4. "New Foreign Books." *Times Literary Supplement* [London, England] 10 Nov. 1921: 735. *Times Literary Supplement* Historical Archive. http://www.the-tls.co.uk/tls/archives/, accessed 22 Apr. 2015. The authorship of the brief reviews of foreign books on this page is unattributed.

friend Franz Marc's famous "Blue Rider" school of painting, and she often expresses her attraction to the unworldly color blue and her affinity with the ground-breaking spirit of her most adventurous contemporaries, a spirit evident in one of her most famously Expressionist poems, "My Blue Piano":

At home I have a blue piano,
I, who cannot play a note.

It stands in the gloom of the cellar door,
now that the whole world has grown coarse.

The four hands of the stars play there
— the moonwife sang in her boat —
and the rats come out to dance.

The keyboard and the works all busted . . . . .
My blubbering enters the blue of death.

O angels, open me your way,
forbidden though it be the living.
I who ate the bitter bread now
call you at the door to heaven.

Friendships with important painters and writers of the era are remembered just before and during World War I in poems to Franz Marc, Franz Werfel, George Grosz, and others. This is the whole of her elegy to Georg Trakl:

Georg Trakl fell in the war, dead by his own hand.
It was that lonely in the world. I loved him.

Hebrew Ballads, also published at this time, tell stories from scripture and take up religious questions important in her later work. Sometimes, the sense of abandonment stirs a spirit of prophecy which, in more declamatory moments, rises into vehemence. But Lasker-Schüler brings this cosmic vision home more often into an experience of vulnerability and transport, as in "The End of the World":

What a weeping in the world,
as if dear God himself had died
and let his leaden shadow fall
like earth into the grave.

Come hide in here with me . . .
life is laid out in the breast
like one of us in a pinewood box.

Quick now, kiss me, here —
such a knocking at the heart
soon leaves any creature senseless.

The pangs of the abandoned soul haunt not only love poems, but poems dedicated to the poet's mother, and maybe most movingly in "To My Child," the elegy to her son, who felt himself largely abandoned by his mother, and who, when he was dying of tuberculosis at twenty-seven, asked that she not be permitted to visit him.

Always you keep dying, child, always you
and the year keep slipping away.

Under the thinning leaves
and branches, you

with the red rose
taste of bitter death.

Not one dying throb of it
is spared you.

Endlessly, I cry . . . . .
in the night, for you my dear, in my heart,

and still that lullaby in my throat,
those sobbing notes I sang you while you died.

These eyes of mine turn no more
to the world;

the green leaves make them sorry.
— But the eternal lives inside me.

Love of you is the image of God
permitted me in this world.

I saw the angels crying too,
in the wind where the wet snow fell.

They hovered . . . .
in a heavenly draft.

The moon in its full flower
calls to mind my child in life.

And now I cannot bear to see
the butterfly float in a sorrowless light.

I never thought how death
kept closing on you, my sweet child.

I love the walls of your room,
where I paint your face in boyhood.

The usual stars that fall
this time of year are burning
this time into my heart.

Some of Lasker-Schüler's best-known lyrics address her most famous lover, the physician and celebrated poet, Gottfried Benn. During their brief involvement, a few years after her second marriage failed, Benn in his twenties was just publishing his first disturbingly fierce book of verse. Lasker-Schüler, in her forties, had published several books of poems and prose. Since Benn did not appear to reciprocate the all-consuming passion that his older and more celebrated lover felt toward him, the differences between them are distinct from the beginning.

Twenty years after they separated, Benn, whose Expressionism was as "decadent" as any, espoused National Socialism at its inception, and even after his early disaffection from the party served in the German medical corps during World War II.

In 1933, a few months after Lasker-Schüler at sixty-three had received the Kleist Prize, one of Germany's highest literary honors, she was assaulted in the street by Nazis. Within hours she fled Germany for Switzerland. Denied residence, she traveled to Alexandria and settled finally in Jerusalem. There she slept sitting up in a small, unheated room without a bed, a vantage she found satisfactory during her final years, she said, because from her window she saw beyond the graveyards the mountains of Moab. Haunted by the murder of her people in the land of her childhood, she wrote "The One They Frightened Away":

The whole day wrapped in fog,
where worlds in limbo meet —
mere shadow puppets of themselves.

How long, my heart, since any kindness . . .
since this world grew cold, and people faded.
Come, the two of us, let's pray. God comforts me.

Where is the living breath once mine?
I pass among the drifting herds of deer
as faintly as a dream — yes, I did love you . . . .

Where shall I go when the north wind roars
with ice? Shy creatures of the wild make way,
and at your door my flower, soft as mullein.

Soon my tears will wash away the very stars
from heaven. At this cup the poet's thirst
took ease—as did you, and I.

Her last poems are all the more moving when we consider the circumstance of their composition: with the poet, in exile, soon to die, and her people in the camps, suffering from the deadly cold of winds that are not metaphorical, as here in "Fall":

The one last daisy by the path I pick for me . . . . .
An angel came to stitch my burial clothes —
I must be next, it seems, in another world.

Eternal life to those who speak much love.
Those born in love can only rise again!
Hate shuts the pit! high though the flare may burn.

And much I wish to speak to you, much love —
though cold winds reel by now
around the trees, around the hearts
that in their cradles lay.

Trouble was my portion in the world . . . . .
The moon gives answer to your questionings,
the moon who saw me on those cloudy days
when I went tiptoe still, and faint of heart.

The poet in Jerusalem during the war was still, in her seventies, a famous eccentric. Amichai remembers her fondly from his youth, dressed in an outlandish fur hat in the heat of summer, and bedecked with costume jewelry.[5] Some have said that she was psychologically unhinged by paranoia at the end of her life. For the distress in poverty of an old woman driven from her homeland by thugs and mocked by local children in her place of exile, paranoia may not be the term of art. In any case, although she died from heart failure before the final defeat of the Nazi regime, her vision of the redemptive power of love is as potent as ever in this, one of her last poems, "A Lovesong":

Come to me in the night, and in love's tangle shall we
 sleep,
weary as I am, from wakeful nights alone.
Already in the dark of dawn a strange bird made its cry,
my dream still wrestling with itself and me.

By the wellsprings flowers open,
everlastings with blue eyes . . . . .

Come to me in the night in slippers worn by the seven stars,
and wrapped in veils of love — come late, and quiet, into
 my tent,

5. *Selected Poems*, Else Lasker-Schüler, trans. Audri Durchslag-Litt, with an introduction by Yehuda Amichai (Los Angeles: Green Integer, 2000).

as moons bestir themselves out of the dusty casks of
heaven.

We two shall take our rest in love, like creatures all but
vanished,
curled in a nest in the high bamboo beyond the reach of
the world.

My Blue Piano

Trieb

Es treiben mich brennende Lebensgewalten,
Gefühle, die ich nicht zügeln kann,
Und Gedanken, die sich zur Form gestalten,
Fallen mich wie Wölfe an!

Ich irre durch duftende Sonnentage . . .
Und die Nacht erschüttert von meinem Schrei.
Meine Lust stöhnt wie eine Marterklage
Und reisst sich von ihrer Fessel frei.

Und schwebt auf zitternden, schimmernden Schwingen
Dem sonn'gen Thal in den jungen Schoss,
Und läßt sich von jedem Mai'nhauch bezwingen
Und giebt der Natur sidt willenlos.

1902

Drive

What fire drives me feeds bone-deep —
feelings thought cannot restrain,
thoughts that take shape after dark
like wolves and harry me toward dawn.

I blunder through the days of incense,
shaken under night's duress,
and feel the soul's urge like a martyr
crying tear free from her jess.

And swim on the quaking of her wings
into the lap of a sunlit vale,
and overcome by the smallest wind
yield for pleasure her least will.

Urfrühling

Sie trug eine Schlange als Gürtel
Und Paradiesäpfel auf dem Hut,
Und meine wilde Sehnsucht
Raste weiter in ihrem Blut.

Und das Ursonnenbangen,
Das Schwermüt'ge der Glut
Und die Blässe meiner Wangen
Standen auch ihr so gut.

Das war ein Spiel der Geschicke
Ein's ihrer Rätseldinge . . .
Wir senkten zitternd die Blicke
In die Märchen unserer Ringe.

Ich vergass meines Blutes Eva
Ueber all' diesen Seelenlklippen,
Und es brannte das Rot ihres Mundes,
Als hätte ich Knabenlippen.

Und das Abendröten glühte
Sich schlängelnd am Himmelssaume,
Und vom Erkenntnisbaume
Lächelte spottgut die Blüte.

1902

Eve's Persuasion

She wrapped a snake around her hips
and wore passionfruit on her head,
and my unspoken yearnings
whispered further in her blood.

The ancient trouble in the sun,
the heavy-heartedness of hot coals,
and the pallor of my cheeks
all burgeoned in her soul.

It was a play of Fate,
a pas de deux of wills . . .
when we looked trembling down
at each other's jewels.

On that cliff's edge I forgot
the innocence lost in my blood,
and the red of her mouth now burned
at my lips as if she were my bride.

And the red streaks in the evening sky
wrapped the fringe of the woods,
and from the Tree of Knowledge
burst the mockery of the buds.

Dann

. . . Dann kam die Nacht mit Deinem Traum
Im stillen Sternebrennen.
Und der Tag zog lächelnd an mir vorbei,
Und die wilden Rosen atmeten kaum.

Nun sehn' ich mich nach Traumesmai,
Nach Deinem Liebeoffenbaren.
Möchte an Deinem Munde brennen
Eine Traumzeit von tausend Jahren.

1902

Then

. . . Then came nighttime with your dream
under the still fire of the stars,
and daylight on its way by beamed
and held its breath in the sweetbriers.

Now I long to dream in the time
of love's unfolding flame,
when my fire finds your dreaming mouth
in flower for a thousand years.

Sinnenrausch

Dein sünd'ger Mund ist meine Totengruft,
Betäubend ist sein süsser Atemduft,
Denn meine Tugenden entschliefen.
Ich trinke sinnberauscht aus seiner Quelle
Und sinke willenlos in ihre Tiefen,
Verklärten Blickes in die Hölle.

Mein heisser Leib erglüht in seinem Hauch,
Er zittert, wie ein junger Rosenstrauch,
Geküsst vom warmen Maienregen.
— Ich folge Dir ins wilde Land der Sünde
Und pflücke Feuerlilien auf den Wegen,
— Wenn ich die Heimat auch nicht wiederfinde . . .

1902

Love-Drunk

Your wicked mouth is my death chamber.
Stunned by the sweetness of its breath,
with all my virtues put to sleep,
I drink from its narcotic well
and sink unwilling through its depth,
gaze radiant, into hell.

My thighs burn where you breathe.
They tremble like rosebushes in first bud
under a warm touch from the rain.
— I follow in the bewildering gloom
and pluck fire lilies by the road,
— though few who go this way come home.

Sein Blut

Am liebsten pflückte er meines Glückes
Letzte Rose im Maien
Und würfe sie in den Rinnstein.
. . . Sein Blut plagt ihn.

Am liebsten lockte er meiner Seele
Zitternden Sonnenstrahl
In seine düst're Nächtequal.

Am liebsten griff er mein spielendes Herz
Aus wiegendem Lenzhauch
Und hing es auf wo an einem Dornstrauch.
. . . Sein Blut plagt ihn.

1902

His Blood

What might suit him is to cast
my happiness's last young rose
into the gutter like bad dice.
. . . His blood bores him.

What might suit him is to draw
the least flickering of my soul
into the blear pit of a yawn.

What might suit him is to pluck
the hatchling from joy's nest
and hang it in a thornbush.
. . . His blood bores him.

Viva!

Mein Wünschen sprudelt in der Sehnsucht meines Blutes
Wie wilder Wein, der zwischen Feuerblättern glüht.
Ich wollte, Du und ich, wir wären eine Kraft,
Wir wären eines Blutes
Und ein Erfüllen, eine Leidenschaft,
Ein heisses Weltenliebeslied!

Ich wollte, Du und ich, wir würden uns verzweigen,
Wenn sonnentoll der Sommertag nach Regen schreit
Und Wetterwolken bersten in der Luft!
Und alles Leben wäre unser Eigen;
Den Tod selbst rissen wir aus seiner Gruft
Und jubelten durch seine Schweigsamkeit!

Ich wollte, dass aus unserer Kluft sich Massen
Wie Felsen aufeinandertürmen und vermünden
In einen Gipfel, unerreichbar weit!
Dass wir das Herz des Himmels ganz erfassen
Und uns in jedem Hauche finden
Und überstrahlen alle Ewigkeit!

Ein Feiertag, an dem wir ineinanderrauschen,
Wir beide ineinanderstürzen werden,
Wie Quellen, die aus steiler Felshöh' sich ergiessen
In Wellen, die dem eignen Singen lauschen
Und plötzlich niederbrausen und zusammenfliessen
In unzertrennbar, wilden Wasserheerden!

1902

Viva!

My wishes spurt forth into my yearning blood
the way wild vines seethe over a bough in flames.
I want the two of us made one,
one force, one blood, one fullness,
you and I made one long agony,
one world-consuming song of arrant love!

I want your branchings woven into mine,
when sun-crazed summer cries out loud
for rain, and bursts the thunderhead!
Life's force belongs to us, and death
we drag forth from his arid vault
and laugh back into the silence!

I want cliffs risen from our abyss
to overtop each other past
the topmost mountain and beyond!
hearts grappled to the heart of heaven
where we feel our power in the wind
and outshine even the unending!

Heedless, surging into the headlong
overflow, we fall inside each other
down steep faces, gushes listening
only to themselves where suddenly
downroaring into one wild prime
unshorn we braid the waterfall!

Chaos

Die Sterne fliehen schreckensbleich
Vom Himmel meiner Einsamkeit,
Und das schwarze Auge der Mitternacht
Starrt näher und näher.

Ich finde mich nicht wieder
In dieser Todverlassenheit!
Mir ist: ich lieg' von mir weltenweit
Zwischen grauer Nacht der Urangst . . .

Ich wollte, ein Schmerzen rege sich
Und stürze mich grausam nieder
Und riß mich jäh an mich!
Und es lege eine Schöpferlust
Mich wieder in meine Heimat
    Unter der Mutterbrust.

Meine Mutterheimat ist seeleleer,
Es blühen dort keine Rosen
Im warmen Odem mehr. —
. . . . Möcht einen Herzallerliebsten haben!
Und mich in seinem Fleisch vergraben.

1902

Chaos

The stars go dim with fear and flee
into the night of my sole yearning,
and the empty eye of the deep
pores over my forlornness.

No longer can I find myself
in this death-emptied gray!
A world apart I seem to lie
in the pristine night of anguish . . .

If only hurt could stir,
I wish, and plunge me
into a suffering self,
for a god of pleasure
to ferry me home
        under my mother's breast!

My motherland is soulless.
No rose blooms
in the tepid air. —
. . . . But o! that my heart's most tender love
could bury me in his flesh.

Weltschmerz

Ich, der brennende Wüstenwind,
Erkaltete und nahm Gestalt an.

Wo ist die Sonne, die mich auflösen kann,
Oder der Blitz, der mich zerschmettern kann!

Blick nun, ein steinernes Sphinxhaupt,
Zürnend zu allen Himmeln auf.

1902

Weltschmerz

Out of the hot noon blast I grew
cooler and more shapely.

What sun's fire could ever melt my ice,
what mere thunderbolt could crack me!

Look: a stone-eyed sphinx head
sulks back into heaven.

Fortissimo

Du spieltest ein ungestümes Lied,
Ich fürchtete mich nach dem Namen zu fragen,
Ich wusste, er würde das alles sagen,
Was zwischen uns wie Lava glüht.

Da mischte sich die Natur hinein
In unsere stumme Herzensgeschichte,
Der Mondvater lachte mit Vollbackenschein,
Als machte er komische Liebesgedichte.

Wir lachten heimlich im Herzensgrund,
Doch unsere Augen standen in Thränen
Und die Farben des Teppichs spielten bunt
In Regenbogenfarbentönen.

Wir hatten beide dasselbe Gefühl,
Der Smyrnateppich wäre ein Rasen,
Und die Palmen über uns fächelten kühl,
Und unsere Sehnsucht begann zu rasen.

Und unsere Sehnsucht riss sich los
Und jagte uns mit Blutsturmwellen:
Wir sanken in das Smyrnamoos
Urwild und schrieen wie Gazellen.

1902

Fortissimo

You played me an unbridled song.
I dared not ask the name
for fear that it would tell
what lava touched us with its flame.

Our hearts' essence blended,
notwithstanding my demur,
which made the full moon laugh
as if he were lust's puppeteer.

And we too laughed a hidden laugh
while tears stood in our eyes,
and the carpet swirled about us
with the rainbow's potencies.

We felt it both the same:
the Smyrna carpet seemed a lawn
and palms in the cool above us wafted
while our blood began to burn.

And when our yearning tore away
and broke back onto us in swells,
we sank into the Smyrna moss
gone wild and screaming like gazelles.

Dir

Drum wein ich,
Daß bei deinem Kuß
Ich so nichts empfinde
Und ins Leere versinken muß.
Tausend Abgründe
Sind nicht so tief,
Wie diese große Leere.
Ich sinne im engsten Dunkel der Nacht,
Wie ich dirs ganz leise sage,
Doch ich habe nicht den Mut.
Ich wollte, es käme ein Südenwind,
Der dirs herübertrage,
Damit es nicht gar voll Kälte kläng
Und er dirs warm in die Seele säng
Kaum merklich durch dein Blut.

1902

Answer

I cannot tell you
how I sink
to find your kiss
gone empty.
No abyss
could drown the lack,
and in the narrow night
I think how
one might
tell you gently.
I cannot.
But, if it could,
I'd let a south wind
bear some warmer
inkling
to your blood.

Traum

Der Schlaf entführte mich in deine Gärten,
In deinen Traum — die Nacht war wolkenschwarz
umwunden —
Wie düstere Erden starrten deine Augenrunden,
Und deine Blicke waren Härten —

Und zwischen uns lag eine weite, steife
Tonlose Ebene . . .
Und meine Sehnsucht, hingegebene,
Küßt deinen Mund, die blassen Lippenstreife.

1905

Dream

Sleep was a ravishment on your lawn,
as if you dreamed me in my dream:
the night sky shrouded black, your eyeballs
bulging like dead worlds,

and only an empty stage between us
at the interlude gone toneless . . .
and my yearning given way,
I kissed the gray streak of your lips.

Mein Stilles Lied

Mein Herz ist eine traurige Zeit,
Die tonlos tickt.

Meine Mutter hatte goldene Flügel,
Die keine Welt fanden.

Horcht, mich sucht meine Mutter,
Lichte sind ihre Finger und ihre Füße wandernde Träume.

Und süße Wetter mit blauen Wehen
Wärmen meine Schlummer

Immer in den Nächten,
Deren Tage meiner Mutter Krone tragen.

Und ich trinke aus dem Monde stillen Wein,
Wenn die Nacht einsam kommt.

Meine Lieder trugen des Sommers Bläue
Und kehrten düster heim.

— Ihr verhöhntet meine Lippe
Und redet mit ihr. —

Doch ich griff nach euren Händen,
Denn meine Liebe ist ein Kind und wollte spielen.

Und ich artete mich nach euch,
Weil ich mich nach dem Menschen sehnte.

Arm bin ich geworden
An eurer bettelnden Wohltat.

Und das Meer wird es wehklagen
Gott.

My Quiet Song

My heart is an unhappy hour
ticking with no sound.

My mother's golden wings keep searching
into the world, and finding

neither it nor me, rummaging in the quiet,
candles for fingers, listless dreams for feet.

Yet always sweet blue winds
are warming me in the night,

and days wear
every day again my mother's crown.

When night comes back alone,
I drink wine mute from the moon.

My songs have borne the summer blue
and gone home dark.

And you who scorned me,
whispering at my lip,

I would have taken your hands, for my love
is a child that wants to play.

Yet I am become as you,
from yearning after the ways of men,

my heart made poor
by begging you your mercy.

Thus have the seas cried woe
to the heavens.

Ich bin der Hieroglyph,
Der unter der Schöpfung steht

Und mein Auge
Ist der Gipfel der Zeit;

Sein Leuchten küßt Gottes Saum.

1905

I am the hieroglyph
marked in the tablet of being.

This eye
is the mountaintop of time.

This shining
touches God at his hem.

Mein Liebeslied

Wie ein heimlicher Brunnen
Murmelt mein Blut,
Immer von dir, immer von mir.

Unter dem taumelnden Mond
Tanzen meine nackten, suchenden Träume,
Nachtwandelnde Kinder,
Leise über düstere Hecken.

O, deine Lippen sind sonnig . . .
Diese Rauschedüfte deiner Lippen . . .
Und aus blauen Dolden silberumringt
Lächelst du . . . du, du.

Immer das schlängelnde Geriesel
Auf meiner Haut
Über die Schulter hinweg —
Ich lausche . . .

Wie ein heimlicher Brunnen
Murmelt mein Blut.

1905

My Lovesong

Wellings homeborn in my blood
murmur me always, always you.

Under the staggering moon
my naked dreams go dancing, searching,
children who sleepwalk softly
beyond the gloom of the hedgerows.

O, but your lips, your sunwarm
drunken scented lips . . . all day
from clustered silver-blue-streaked flowers,
you, your lips, you smiling, you.

And always the snakelike rippling
of gooseflesh
over my shoulder down . . .
I listen . . .

Wellings homeborn in my blood
murmur me always, always . . .

Weltende

Es ist ein Weinen in der Welt,
Als ob der liebe Gott gestorben wär,
Und der bleierne Schatten, der niederfällt,
Lastet grabesschwer.

Komm, wir wollen uns näher verbergen . . .
Das Leben liegt in aller Herzen
Wie in Särgen.

Du! wir wollen uns tief küssen —
Es pocht eine Sehnsucht an die Welt,
An der wir sterben müssen.

1905

The End of the World

What a weeping in the world,
as if dear God himself had died
and let his leaden shadow fall
like earth into the grave.

Come hide in here with me . . .
life is laid out in the breast
like one of us in a pinewood box.

Quick now, kiss me, here —
such a knocking at the heart
soon leaves any creature senseless.

Ein Alter Tibetteppich

Deine Seele, die die meine liebet,
Ist verwirkt mit ihr im Teppichtibet.

Strahl in Strahl, verliebte Farben,
Sterne, die sich himmellang umwarben.

Unsere Füße ruhen auf der Kostbarkeit,
Maschentausendabertausendweit.

Süßer Lamasohn auf Moschuspflanzenthron,
Wie lange küßt dein Mund den meinen wohl
Und Wang die Wange buntgeknüpfte Zeiten schon?

1911

An Old Tibetan Rug

Your soul by loving mine has woven us
into this old Tibetan rug,

as love unspooling from the stars weaves
heaven from various threads of light.

And you, feet touching this bright heirloom
with its weft of a thousand colors,

my sweet Lama on your muskwood throne,
how long can your mouth finding mine
braid lip and lip in the carpet of time?

Heimweh

Ich kann die Sprache
Dieses kühlen Landes nicht,
Und seinen Schritt nicht gehn.

Auch die Wolken, die vorbeiziehn,
Weiß ich nicht zu deuten.

Die Nacht ist eine Stiefkönigin.

Immer muß ich an die Pharaonenwälder denken
Und küsse die Bilder meiner Sterne.

Meine Lippen leuchten schon
Und sprechen Fernes,

Und bin ein buntes Bilderbuch
Auf deinem Schoß.

Aber dein Antlitz spinnt
Einen Schleier aus Weinen.

Meinen schillernden Vögeln
Sind die Korallen ausgestochen,

An den Hedeen der Gärten
Versteinern sich ihre weichen Nester.

Wer salbt meine toten Paläste —
Sie trugen die Kronen meiner Väter,
Ihre Gebete versanken im heiligen Fluß.

1911

Homesick

The speech of this
cold country is not mine.
Nor can I keep the pace.

Even the clouds
escape me.

Night here is a foisted queen.

And still I bear in mind
wild places Pharaohs ride.
I kiss the likeness
of Egyptian stars.

My lips shine
from outlandishness,

and I am the picturebook
glistening in your lap.

But tears weave silk
threads down your face.

My opalescent birds
with enlaid coral gouged away

in garden hedges feel
their soft nests turning into stone.

And those who anointed the palace of my dead,
they carried the crowns of my fathers,
prayers they sang at the holy river sank.

Meine Mutter

War sie der große Engel,
Der neben mir ging?

Oder liegt meine Mutter begraben
Unter dem Himmel von Rauch —
Nie blüht es blau über ihrem Tode.

Wenn meine Augen doch hell schienen
Und ihr Licht brächten.

Wäre mein Lächeln nicht versunken im Antlitz,
Ich würde es über ihr Grab hängen.

Aber ich weiß einen Stern,
Auf dem immer Tag ist;
Den will ich über ihre Erde tragen.

Ich werde jetzt immer ganz allein sein
Wie der große Engel,
Der neben mir ging.

1911

My Mother

Was she the tall one, the angel
that walked beside me?

Or has my mother been buried
in smoke — where the blue flower
cannot open.

If only these living eyes
could bring her light.

If the smile were not sunk in my face,
I might hang it here on her stone.

I do know a star
where day shines always;
this shall I lift up over her grave.

Now I am always alone
like the tall one, the angel
who walked beside me.

Marie von Nazareth

Träume, säume, Marienmädchen —
Überall löscht der Rosenwind
Die schwarzen Sterne aus.
Wiege im Arme dein Seelchen.

Alle Kinder kommen auf Lämmern
Zottehotte geritten,
Gottlingchen sehen —

Und die vielen Schimmerblumen
An den Hecken —
Und den großen Himmel da
Im kurzen Blaukleide!

1911

Mary of Nazareth

Dreamer, dawdler, young maid Mary,
everywhere a wind from the roses
quenching the black, black stars —
cradle in your arms that peeping soul.

All the children are coming on lambs,
toddler on toddler
to see the godling.

Hedges overflow
with blossom,
and all that vastness wrapped
in a little blue shirt!

Versöhnung

Es wird ein großer Stern in meinen Schoß fallen . . .
Wir wollen wachen die Nacht,

In den Sprachen beten,
Die wie Harfen eingeschnitten sind.

Wir wollen uns versöhnen die Nacht —
So viel Gott strömt über.

Kinder sind unsere Herzen,
Die möchten ruhen müdesüß.

Und unsere Lippen wollen sich küssen,
Was zagst du?

Grenzt nicht mein Herz an deins —
Immer färbt dein Blut meine Wangen rot.

Wir wollen uns versöhnen die Nacht,
Wenn wir uns herzen, sterben wir nicht.

Es wird ein großer Stern in meinen Schoß fallen.

1911

Reconciliation

Into my loins a star is soon to fall . . .
Come watch with me tonight,

and pray in the tongues
they carve into the wood of the harp.

May we make peace between us through the night —
God wells up to overflowing.

Our two hearts are children
wishing each the other such sweet rest

our lips want only that we kiss.
And why do you hold back?

Does my heart not lie next to yours?
Your blood blushes in my cheeks.

May we make peace between us in the night,
we shall not die if we embrace.

Into my loins a star is soon to fall.

Mein Volk

Der Fels wird morsch,
Dem ich entspringe
Und meine Gotteslieder singe . . .
Jäh stürz ich vom Weg
Und riesele ganz in mir
Fernab, allein fiber Klagegestein
Dem Meer zu.

Hab mich so abgeströmt
Von meines Blutes
Mostvergorenheit.
Und immer, immer noch der Widerhall
In mir,
Wenn schauerlich gen Ost
Das morsche Felsgebein,
Mein Volk,
Zu Gott schreit.

1905

My People

The rock is weathering
whence I flow
and sing my songs of God . . .
I plunge headlong from the path
and shimmer inside myself
away, muttering stone by stone
my sole complaint to the sea.

I poured away so much
of the young wine sparkling
in my blood . . .
Always and forever
songs re-echoing
inside me, tremulous
the downpour easterly
over the broken ribs of stone,
my people cry
to God.

Pharao und Joseph

Pharao verstößt seine blühenden Weiber,
Sie duften nach den Gärten Amons.

Sein Königskopf ruht auf meiner Schulter,
Die strömt Korngeruch aus.

Pharao ist von Gold.
Seine Augen gehen und kommen
Wie schillernde Nilwellen.

Sein Herz aber liegt in meinem Blut;
Zehn Wölfe gingen an meine Tränke.

Immer denkt Pharao
An meine Brüder,
Die mich in die Grube warfen.

Säulen werden im Schlaf seine Arme
Und drohen!

Aber sein träumerisch Herz
Rauscht auf meinem Grund.

Darum dichten meine Lippen
Große Süßigkeiten,
Im Weizen unseres Morgens.

1905

Pharaoh and Joseph

Pharaoh rebukes his burgeoning wives,
their passing fragrant as the day through gardens.

He lays his kingly head on my shoulder,
fresh with scent of wheat.

All of gold is Pharaoh, eyes
whose kingship comes and goes
like glimmerings on the Nile.

Within my blood, though, lies his heart.
Ten wolves drank at the springs of my well.

Always Pharaoh remembers
my brothers
who cast me into the wellshaft.

His arms like pillars
in his sleep
loom over them.

His heart keeps rushing
in the dream along a bank
whose very earth I am.

My lips draw thence
into their speech such sweetness
as the summer wheat at daybreak.

Moses und Josua

Als Moses im Alter Gottes war,
Nahm er den wilden Juden Josua
Und salbte ihn zum König seiner Schar.

Da ging ein Sehnen weich durch Israel —
Denn Josuas Herz erquickte wie ein Quell.
Des Bibelvolkes Judenleib war sein Altar.

Die Mägde mochten den gekrönten Bruder gern —
Wie heiliger Dornstrauch brannte süß sein Haar;
Sein Lächeln grüßte den ersehnten Heimatstern,

Den Mosis altes Sterbeauge aufgehn sah,
Als seine müde Löwenseele schrie zum Herrn.

1913

Moses and Joshua

When Moses was the age of God,
he took the wild Jew Joshua
and dubbed him king of all the tribes.

Then a gentle yearning flowed through Israel
from Joshua's quickening heart as from a well.
The body of his people was his ark.

The maidens loved their brother newly crowned —
his hair the sweet flame of the holy bush,
his smile an answer to their yearning star,

which old Moses at his dying yet saw dawn,
the weary lion roaring in his soul to God.

Abraham und Isaak

Abraham baute in der Landschaft Eden
Sich eine Stadt aus Erde und aus Blatt
Und übte sich mit Gott zu reden.

Die Engel ruhten gern vor seiner frommen Hütte
Und Abraham erkannte jeden;
Himmlische Zeichen ließen ihre Flügelschritte.

Bis sie dann einmal bang in ihren Träumen
Meckern hörten die gequälten Böcke,
Mit denen Isaak Opfern spielte hinter Süßholzbäumen.

Und Gott ermahnte: Abraham!!
Er brach vom Kamm des Meeres Muscheln ab und Schwamm
Hoch auf den Blöcken den Altar zu schmücken.

Und trug den einzigen Sohn gebunden auf den Rücken
Zu werden seinem großen Herrn gerecht —
Der aber liebte seinen Knecht.

1913

Abraham and Isaac

Abraham in the land of Eden built a city
all of earth and leaves, and schooled
himself to speak therein with God.

The angels lay at ease about his tent,
whose nature Abraham could read from every
foot- and wing-stroke in the dust.

Then, they heard once in uneasy dreams
the cry of rams, where Isaac used to play
at sacrifice behind the incense trees.

And God called: Abraham!! — his servant,
who from seacombs plucked bright shells
and sponges to bedeck the altar.

Bound on his back he bore his only son
toward where the dread voice told him go,
and God, they say, remembered this with love.

Ein Lied der Liebe

Seit du nicht da bist,
Ist die Stadt dunkel.

Ich sammle die Schatten
Der Palmen auf,
Darunter du wandeltest.

Immer muß ich eine Melodie summen,
Die hängt lächelnd an den Ästen.

Du liebst mich wieder —
Wem soll ich mein Entzücken sagen?

Einer Waise oder einem Hochzeitler,
Der im Widerhall das Glück hört.

Ich weiß immer,
Wann du an mich denkst —

Dann wird mein Herz ein Kind
Und schreit.

An jedem Tor der Straße
Verweile ich und träume;

Ich helfe der Sonne deine Schönheit malen
An allen Wänden der Häuser.

Aber ich magere
An deinem Bilde.

Um schlanke Säulen schlinge ich mich
Bis sie schwanken.

A Song of Love

Without you
the city is dark.

I gather shadows
of palm fronds
where you walked.

And always I have to hum the tune
that shines to me out of the branches.

You love me again —
whom shall I tell my joy.

An orphan maybe, a bridegroom,
might catch the drift of my luck.

I know whenever you hold me
in your thoughts —

my heart becomes a child
and cries.

At every gate along the street
I linger a little and dream.

I help the sun to paint your glow
on the houses.

Still I dwindle, starving myself
on your image.

Around thin columns I coil my length
until I feel them wobble.

Überall steht Wildedel,
Die Blüten unseres Blutes.

Wir tauchen in heilige Moose,
Die aus der Wolle goldener Lämmer sind.

Wenn doch ein Tiger
Seinen Leib streckte

Über die Ferne, die uns trennt,
Wie zu einem nahen Stern.

Auf meinem Angesicht
Liegt früh dein Hauch.

1917

Beyond this city a wilderness
teems in our blood,

toppling us onto moss
more golden than wool of a sacred lamb.

If only a tiger
stretching his limbs

across the distance between us
could stoop as near as a star,

I would feel on my face
the tint of dawn from your breath.

Senna Hoy

Seit du begraben liegst auf dem Hügel,
Ist die Erde süß.

Wo ich hingehe nun auf Zehen,
Wandele ich über reine Wege.

O deines Blutes Rosen
Durchtränken sanft den Tod.

Ich habe keine Furcht mehr
Vor dem Sterben.

Auf deinem Grabe blühe ich schon
Mit den Blumen der Schlingpflanzen.

Deine Lippen haben mich immer gerufen,
Nun weiß mein Name nicht mehr zurück.

Jede Schaufel Erde, die dich barg,
Verschüttete auch mich.

Darum ist immer Nacht an mir,
Und Sterne schon in der Dämmerung.

Und ich bin unbegreiflich unseren Freunden
Und ganz fremd geworden.

Aber du stehst am Tor der stillsten Stadt
Und wartest auf mich, du Großengel.

1917

Senna Hoy

With you lying under the hill
the earth is sweet.

When I go near on tiptoe,
I walk the holiest paths.

Softly the roses of your blood leave
death drenched through and through.

Now I have no fear
of dying.

On your grave I burst
into bloom like a briar.

Your lips have called me always,
and now my name finds no way back.

Every shovelful of earth between us
buries me also.

Night, therefore, is always mine,
and stars already in the dusk.

And I am fathomless to our friends
and am become a stranger.

But you stand at the city gate in the hush
awaiting me, my tall angel.

An den Ritter aus Gold

Du bist alles was aus Gold ist
In der großen Welt.

Ich suche deine Sterne
Und will nicht schlafen.

Wir wollen uns hinter Hecken legen,
Uns niemehr aufrichten.

Aus unseren Händen
Süße Träumerei küssen.

Mein Herz holt sich
Von deinem Munde Rosen.

Meine Augen lieben dich an,
Du haschst nach ihren Faltern.

Was soll ich tun,
Wenn du nicht da bist.

Von meinen Lidern
Tropft schwarzer Schnee;

Wenn ich tot bin,
Spiele du mit meiner Seele.

1917

To the Golden Knight

All there is of gold
in this great world is you.

For you I search the stars
and have no wish to sleep.

We two shall lie down by the hedgerow
never to rise up again.

Let's kiss the sweet stuff
of this daydream from each other's hands.

My heart plucks
roses at your mouth.

From this eye into you love skips;
you track its butterflies.

What shall I do now
when you go.

Black snow
trickles from my lids;

when I am dead,
play this way with my soul.

Giselheer dem Heiden

Ich weine —
Meine Träume fallen in die Welt.

In meine Dunkelheit
Wagt sich kein Hirte.

Meine Augen zeigen nicht den Weg
Wie die Sterne.

Immer bettle ich vor deiner Seele;
Weißt du das?

Wär ich doch blind —
Dächte dann, ich läg in deinem Leib.

Alle Blüten täte ich
Zu deinem Blut.

Ich bin vielreich,
Niemandwer kann mich pflücken;

Oder meine Gaben tragen
Heim.

Ich will dich ganz zart mich lehren;
Schon weißt du mich zu nennen.

Sieh meine Farben,
Schwarz und stern

Und mag den kühlen Tag nicht,
Der hat ein Glasauge.

Giselheer the Heathen

These tears of mine, these dreams . . .
keep falling into the world.

Into that darkness
no good shepherd comes.

Nor can these eyes light up the way
like stars.

And yet I beg you to your soul.
Can you not hear?

Blind — I should have thought
I was laid out under your flesh.

I should have borne my flowerings
into your blood.

For I am rich.
And none can pluck this blossom,

none bear this gift
home.

Yet tenderly shall I teach you
of myself. Already you say my name.

Behold my colors then,
my black, my star,

and the cool day I abhor,
with one glass eye.

Alles ist tot,
Nur du und ich nicht.

1917

All is dead, all dead
but you and me.

Giselheer dem Knaben

An meiner Wimper hängt ein Stern,
Es ist so hell
Wie soll ich schlafen —

Und möchte mit dir spielen.
— Ich habe keine Heimat —
Wir spielen König und Prinz.

1917

Giselheer as a Boy

With a star this bright hung
from the tip of my eyelash
how shall I sleep —

Let me play a little with you.
— I have no homeland —
Let's play King and Prince.

Lauter Diamant

Ich hab in deinem Antlitz
Meinen Sternenhimmel ausgeträumt.

Alle meine bunten Kosenamen
Gab ich dir,

Und legte die Hand
Unter deinen Schritt,

Als ob ich dafür
Ins Jenseits käme.

Immer weint nun
Vom Himmel deine Mutter,

Da ich mich schnitzte
Aus deinem Herzfleische,

Und du so viel Liebe
Launisch verstießest.

Dunkel ist es —
Es flackert nur noch
Das Licht meiner Seele.

1917

Candor of Diamonds

I dreamed to perfection
a firmament in your face —

as if, for naming you
with gaudy lovenames,

for the hand I laid
under the tread of your heel . . .

I might come home
into a sweet hereafter.

Your mother endlessly
cries from behind the sky

to see me slice myself
from the flesh of your heart,

and that much love
you peevishly refuse.

Dark as it is — you see,
that little flickering
is the light of my soul.

Das Lied des Spielprinzen

Wie kann ich dich mehr noch lieben?
Ich sehe den Tieren und Blumen
Bei der Liebe zu.

Küssen sich zwei Sterne,
Oder bilden Wolken ein Bild —
Wir spielten es schon zarter.

Und deine harte Stirne,
Ich kann mich so recht an sie lehnen,
Sitz drauf wie auf einem Giebel.

Und in deines Kinnes Grube
Bau ich mir ein Raubnest —
Bis — du mich aufgefressen hast.

Find dann einmal morgens
Nur noch meine Kniee,
Zwei gelbe Skarabäen für eines Kaisers Ring.

1917

The Song of the Make-Believe Prince

How could I love you better?
I see the beasts,
the flowers lovestruck.

Two stars kiss, the clouds
disport themselves — and we
do what they do more tenderly.

Your brow gone hard,
I lean full into it,
the stoniness a gable where I perch.

I build in the cleft of your chin
a nest of thieves —
and you devour me —

finding that morning
only the scraps of my knees,
like yellow scarabs for a kaiser's ring.

Giselheer dem Tiger

Über dein Gesicht schleichen die Dschungeln.
O, wie du bist!

Deine Tigeraugen sind süß geworden
In der Sonne.

Ich trag dich immer herum
Zwischen meinen Zähnen.

Du mein Indianerbuch,
Wild West,
Siouxhäuptling!

Im Zwielicht schmachte ich
Gebunden am Buxbaumstamm —

Ich kann nicht mehr sein
Ohne das Skalpspiel.

Rote Küsse malen deine Messer
Auf meine Brust —

Bis mein Haar an deinem Gürtel flattert.

1917

Giselheer the Tiger

Jungles lurk in the shifting dark
of your looks. And how you look!

Those sweet eyes of a tiger
ripen under the sun.

Wherever I go I carry you
in my teeth. You

wild west you,
you book of Indian lore,
Sioux chief!

Bound to the box tree
languishing in the dusk,

I cannot do without
our make-believe of taking scalps.

Your knives leave bright red kisses
on my breast —

until my hair is fluttering from your belt.

O Gott

Überall nur kurzer Schlaf
Im Mensch, im Grün, im Kelch der Winde.
Jeder kehrt in sein totes Herz heim.

— Ich wollt die Welt wär noch ein Kind —
Und wüßte mir vom ersten Atem zu erzählen.

Früher war eine große Frömmigkeit am Himmel,
Gaben sich die Sterne die Bibel zu lesen.
Könnte ich einmal Gottes Hand fassen
Oder den Mond an seinem Finger sehn.

O Gott, o Gott, wie weit bin ich von dir!

1917

O God

Only a short nap, everywhere,
in the mind, in the green woods,
in the grail of the winds. Everyone
turns in the dead of his heart toward home.

— I wish the world were still a child —
and could give me the gospel of her first breath.

There used to be such holiness all through heaven,
they passed the Bible from star to star
to read. If only I could catch God's hand
just once, or see the moon on his finger. God,

how far I am, o God, how far from you!

Höre

Ich raube in den Nächten
Die Rosen deines Mundes,
Daß keine Weibin Trinken findet.

Die dich umarmt,
Stiehlt mir von meinen Schauern,
Die ich um deine Glieder malte.

Ich bin dein Wegrand.
Die dich streift,
Stürzt ab.

Fühlst du mein Lebtum
Überall
Wie ferner Saum?

1917

Listen

In the night I steal
the roses of your mouth
no other woman then may find to drink.

Whoever else may hold you
robs me of my tremblings
which I spend about your thighs.

I am the lip of the path.
The woman whose touch now glides
around you only falls away.

Do you feel my body's realm hold
everywhere
in the forgotten seams?

Verinnerlicht

Ich denke immer ans Sterben,
Mich hat niemand lieb.

Ich wollt ich wär still Heiligenbild
Und alles in mir ausgelöscht.

Träumerisch färbte Abendrot
Meine Augen wund verweint.

Weiß nicht wo ich hin soll
Wie überall zu dir.

Bist meine heimliche Heimat
Und will nichts Leiseres mehr.

Wie blühte ich gern süß empor
An deinem Herzen himmelblau —

Lauter weiche Wege
Legte ich um dein pochend Haus.

1917

Inward, into the Light

I keep my death in mind.
None loves me.

I should be an image peaceful
on the altar, bad fire quenched.

But this dreamy sunset tinges me
red-raw with tears.

And who knows where to turn
when everywhere it's you.

To me your hiddenness is home,
and I want nothing more.

How gladly I would bloom
into the blue sky at your heart.

I lay my open paths at ease
around your throbbing house.

Nur Dich

Der Himmel trägt im Wolkengürtel
Den gebogenen Mond.

Unterdem Sichelbild
Will ich in deiner Hand ruhn.

Immer muß ich wie der Sturm will,
Bin ein Meer ohne Strand.

Aber seit du meine Muscheln suchst,
Leuchtet mein Herz.

Das liegt auf meinem Grund
Verzaubert.

Vielleicht ist mein Herz die Welt,
Pocht —

Und sucht nur noch dich —
Wie soll ich dich rufen?

1917

You Only

The sky on her belt of clouds has hung
the drawn bow of the moon.

Under the sign of the sickle
I want to make my restingplace in your hand.

What the storm bids always must I do,
who am a shoreless sea.

But since you gather cowries from my floor
my heart grows bright

and lies at the bottom
spellbound.

Maybe my heart is the world,
which beats —

which seeks out only you —
how should I call you?

Dem Barbaren

Ich liege in den Nächten
Auf deinem Angesicht.

Auf deines Leibes Steppe
Pflanze ich Zedern und Mandelbäume.

Ich wühle in deiner Brust unermüdlich
Nach den goldenen Freuden Pharaos.

Aber deine Lippen sind schwer,
Meine Wunder erlösen sie nicht.

Hebe doch deine Schneehimmel
Von meiner Seele —

Deine diamantnen Träume
Schneiden meine Adern auf.

Ich bin Joseph und trage einen süßen Gürtel
Um meine bunte Haut.

Dich beglückt das erschrockene Rauschen
Meiner Muscheln.

Aber dein Herz läßt keine Meere mehr ein.
O du!

1917

Barbarian

Night after night
at the ledge of your face I sleep.

On the moors of your loins I plant
my grove with almond trees and cedar.

Your breast unflaggingly I ransack
for the golden joys of Pharaoh.

But your lips are stone,
my wonders work them no release.

Lift off your snowcloud
from my soul —

The diamond teeth of your dreams
tear through my veins.

I am Joseph, girding my brilliant skin
with his sweet raiment.

The frightened roar of my conch
excites you.

You, whose heart
the ocean cannot find.

Dem Herzog von Leipzig

Deine Augen sind gestorben;
Du warst so lange auf dem Meer.

Aber auch ich bin
Ohne Strand.

Meine Stirne ist aus Muschel.
Tang und Seestern hängen an mir.

Einmal möchte ich mit meiner ziellosen Hand
Über dein Gesicht fassen,

Oder eine Eidechse über deine Lippen
Liebentlang mich kräuseln.

Weihrauch strömt aus deiner Haut,
Und ich will dich feiern,

Dir bringen meine Gärten,
Überall blüht mein Herz bunt auf.

1917

The Duke of Leipzig

Your eyes, you were so long
at sea, are now defunct.

I too remain
without a seashore.

My brow is mother-of-pearl.
Kelp and starfish cling to me.

Once with my listless hand
I might have searched your face.

Or curled my lizard length to sleep,
lovingly on your lips.

A smoldering of myrrh pours off your skin,
and I would be the priest

to bear you into the orchards
where the shining of my heart's bloom opens.

Du Machst Mich Traurig — Hör

Bin so müde.
Alle Nächte trag ich auf dem Rücken
Auch deine Nacht,
Die du so schwer umträumst.

Hast du mich lieb?
Ich blies dir arge Wolken von der Stirn
Und tat ihr blau.

Was tust du mir in meiner Todesstunde?

1917

You Who Leave Me Sad, Now Listen

Such a weariness.
Every night I carry on my back
your night as well,
dreamladen with your trouble.

Do you love me?
I swept stormclouds from your brow
and made blue sky.

And you, in the hour of my death, do what?

Abschied

Aber du kamst nie mit dem Abend —
Ich saß im Sternenmantel.

. . . Wenn es an mein Haus pochte,
War es mein eigenes Herz.

Das hängt nun an jedem Türpfosten,
Auch an deiner Tür;

Zwischen Farren verloschende Feuerrose
Im Braun der Guirlande.

Ich färbte dir den Himmel brombeer
Mit meinem Herzblut.

Aber du kamst nie mit dem Abend —
. . . Ich stand in goldenen Schuhen.

1917

Leave-Taking

But you never did come with the evening —
I sat in a robe of stars.

. . . What knocked at the gate
was only my heart.

It hangs from every doorpost now,
from your door too;

fire-roses sombered between fronds
into the brown of the garland.

You I painted with heart's blood
into a blackberry sky.

But you never did come with the evening —
. . . I stood in golden shoes.

Ein Lied

Hinter meinen Augen stehen Wasser,
Die muß ich alle weinen.

Immer möcht ich auffliegen,
Mit den Zugvögeln fort;

Buntatmen mit den Winden
In der großen Luft.

O ich bin so traurig — — — —
Das Gesicht im Mond weiß es.

Drum ist viel samtne Andacht
Und nahender Frühmorgen um mich.

Als an deinem steinernen Herzen
Meine Flügel brachen,

Fielen die Amseln wie Trauerrosen
Hoch vom blauen Gebüsch.

Alles verhaltene Gezwitscher
Will wieder jubeln,

Und ich möchte auffliegen
Mit den Zugvögeln fort.

1917

A Song

Behind these eyes stand waters
all of which I have to weep,

I, who wished to fly forever
among birds of passage south,

breath brilliant as the wind
in open space.

How weary I am now — — — —
the face of the moon well knows.

Velvet unction, therefore,
and pre-dawn contain me.

On your stony heart
my wings have broken.

Blackbirds from the tall blue bush
have fallen, deathlier than roses.

All the twitter they withheld
is wishing somehow to be glad,

and I myself still wish to fly
among the birds of passage south.

Georg Trakl

Georg Trakl erlag im Krieg von eigener Hand gefällt.
So einsam war es in der Welt. Ich hatt ihn lieb.

1917

Georg Trakl

Georg Trakl fell in the war, dead by his own hand.
It was that lonely in the world. I loved him.

Georg Trakl

Seine Augen standen ganz fern.
Er war als Knabe einmal schon im Himmel.

Darum kamen seine Worte hervor
Auf blauen und auf weißen Wolken.

Wir stritten über Religion,
Aber immer wie zwei Spielgefährten,

Und bereiteten Gott von Mund zu Mund.
Im Anfang war das Wort.

Des Dichters Herz, eine feste Burg,
Seine Gedichte: Singende Thesen.

Er war wohl Martin Luther.

Seine dreifaltige Seele trug er in der Hand,
Als er in den heiligen Krieg zog.

— Dann wußte ich, er war gestorben —

Sein Schatten weilte unbegreiflich
Auf dem Abend meines Zimmers.

1917

Georg Trakl

His eyes forever held the distance.
As a boy once he had gone to heaven.

Thus his words came
on blue clouds, and white.

We wrangled over points of faith,
but like playmates,

and made ready, tongue by tongue, for God.
In the beginning was the Word.

The heart of the poet: a mighty fortress.
Poems: theses sung.

He was Martin Godalmighty Luther.

He bore in his hand the triune soul
as if to holy war.

— Then I knew that he was dead —

his shadow inescapably lingered
in my room at dusk.

George Grosz

Manchmal spielen bunte Tränen
In seinen äschernen Augen.

Aber immer begegnen ihm Totenwagen,
Die verscheuchen seine Libellen.

Er ist abergläubig —
— Ward unter einem großen Stern geboren —

Seine Schrift regnet,
Seine Zeichnung: Trüber Buchstabe.

Wie lange im Fluß gelegen,
Blähen seine Menschen sich auf.

Mysteriöse Verlorene mit Quappenmäulern
Und verfaulten Seelen.

Fünf träumende Totenfahrer
Sind seine silbernen Finger.

Aber nirgendwo ein Licht im verirrten Märchen
Und doch ist er ein Kind,

Der Held aus dem Lederstrumpf
Mit dem Indianerstamm auf Duzfuß.

Sonst haßt er alle Menschen,
Sie bringen ihm Unglück.

Aber George Grosz liebt sein Mißgeschick
Wie einen anhänglichen Feind.

George Grosz

Sometimes bright tears play
between his ashen lids.

But he feels lucky, happening into a hearse —
it frightens off the dragonflies.

He's superstitious — born
under the prodigy of a star.

His handwriting pours out;
the sketches: cryptic alphabets.

His people, dredged up from the river,
swell inside their skins,

mysterious, forlorn, with eelpout mouths
and putrid souls.

Five hypnotic escorts of the dead, all
silvery, his fingers transpose the world

into a fairy tale with nowhere any light,
and him in his bewilderment a child,

his hero Leatherstocking,
friend of the Indian tribes.

Everyone else he hates,
they bring bad luck.

But George Grosz adores misfortune,
his dear enemy.

Und seine Traurigkeit ist dionysisch,
Schwarzer Champagner seine Klage.

Er ist ein Meer mit verhängtem Mond,
Sein Gott ist nur scheintot.

1917

However sad, his rite is Dionysian,
his outcry black champagne.

He is an ocean lit by the overcast moon,
where God plays possum.

Gebet

Ich suche allerlanden eine Stadt,
Die einen Engel vor der Pforte hat.
Ich trage seinen großen Flügel
Gebrochen schwer am Schulterblatt
Und in der Stirne seinen Stern als Siegel.

Und wandle immer in die Nacht . . .
Ich habe Liebe in die Welt gebracht —
Daß blau zu blühen jedes Herz vermag,
Und hab ein Leben müde mich gewacht,
In Gott gehüllt den dunklen Atemschlag.

O Gott, schließ um mich deinen Mantel fest;
Ich weiß, ich bin im Kugelglas der Rest,
Und wenn der letzte Mensch die Welt vergießt,
Du mich nicht wieder aus der Allmacht läßt
Und sich ein neuer Erdball um mich schließt.

1917

Prayer

I search the cities of the world
for one with an angel at the gate,
whose broken wings I carry
on my shoulderblades, though stooped,
the shining at my brow his star.

I wander always in the night,
I, who bore the world such love
that every heart might bloom sky blue,
who kept so long a sleepless watch,
my breath a dark veil of my God.

Dear Lord, shut fast about me now, about my soul
your cloak. I am a remnant in the glass
soon spilled, like all else in this world.
Yet may you hold me in your might,
a new orb spinning itself around me.

Gott Hör . . .

Um meine Augen zieht die Nacht sich
Wie ein Ring zusammen.
Mein Puls verwandelte das Blut in Flammen
Und doch war alles grau und kalt um mich.

O Gott und bei lebendigem Tage,
Träum ich vom Tod.
Im Wasser trink ich ihn und würge ihn im Brot.
Für meine Traurigkeit gibt es kein Maß auf deiner Waage.

Gott hör . . . In deiner blauen Lieblingsfarbe
Sang ich das Lied von deines Himmels Dach —
Und weckte doch in deinem ewigen Hauche nicht den Tag.
Mein Herz schämt sich vor dir fast seiner tauben Narbe.

Wo ende ich? — O Gott!! Denn in die Sterne,
Auch in den Mond sah ich, in alle deiner Früchte Tal.
Der rote Wein wird schon in seiner Beere schal . . .
Und überall — die Bitternis — in jedem Kerne.

1932

I Cry, O God, to Thee

Night spins rings
around my sleepless eyes.
My pulse converts my blood to flame,
and things go gray and cold around me.

Now, in the fullness of the day,
I dream of death. I drink of my death
in the water. I choke it down in my bread.
My sadness is past measure.

God . . . I cry to your beloved blue:
I sing into the timeless roof —
and wake in heaven no breath of day.
My heart with its numb scar bears my shame.

Where will it end? O God! I look
to the moon, to the stars, to the clustering grapes.
The red wine in its berry has gone stale . . .
and o, what bitterness in the seed.

Abendlied

Auf die jungen Rosensträucher
Fällt vom Himmel weicher Regen,
Und die Welt wird immer reicher.

O mein Gott mein, nur alleine,
Ich verdurste und verweine
In dem Segen.

Engel singen aus den Höhen:
“Heut ist Gottes Namenstag,
Der allweiß hier vom Geschehen . . .”

Und ich kann es nicht verstehen,
Da ich unter seinem Dach
Oft so traurig erwach.

1932

Evensong

Into a fledgling rosebush
falls from heaven the gentle rain
and the world grows richer.

O my God, my own, for thee
none thirsts in all the world
as I who cry among your riches.

Angels sing down from the rainclouds:
"Praise ye now the birth of God,
who foreknew fully all our bygones."

And I cannot understand them,
since I keep awakening here
under God's roof in my sorrow.

Mein Blaues Klavier

Ich habe zu Hause ein blaues Klavier
Und kenne doch keine Note.

Es steht im Dunkel der Kellertür,
Seitdem die Welt verrohte.

Es spielen Sternenhände vier
— Die Mondfrau sang im Boote —
Nun tanzen die Ratten im Geklirr.

Zerbrochen ist die Klaviatür . . . . .
Ich beweine die blaue Tote.

Ach liebe Engel öffnet mir
— Ich aß vom bitteren Brote —
Mir lebend schon die Himmelstür —
Auch wider dem Verbote.

1943

My Blue Piano

At home I have a blue piano,
I, who cannot play a note.

It stands in the gloom of the cellar door,
now that the whole world has grown coarse.

The four hands of the stars play there
— the moonwife sang in her boat —
and the rats come out to dance.

The keyboard and the works all busted . . . . .
My blubbering enters the blue of death.

O angels, open me your way,
forbidden though it be the living.
I who ate the bitter bread now
call you at the door to heaven.

An Mein Kind

Immer wieder wirst du mir
Im scheidenden Jahre sterben, mein Kind,

Wenn das Laub zerfließt
Und die Zweige schmal werden.

Mit den roten Rosen
Hast du den Tod bitter gekostet,

Nicht ein einziges welkendes Pochen
Blieb dir erspart.

Darum weine ich sehr, ewiglich . . . . .
In der Nacht meines Herzens.

Noch seufzen aus mir die Schlummerlieder,
Die dich in den Todesschlaf schluchzten,

Und meine Augen wenden sich nicht mehr
Der Welt zu;

Das Grün des Laubes tut ihnen weh.
— Aber der Ewige wohnt in mir.

Die Liebe zu dir ist das Bildnis,
Das man sich von Gott machen darf.

Ich sah auch die Engel im Weinen,
Im Wind und im Schneeregen.

Sie schwebten . . . .
In einer himmlischen Luft.

To My Child

Always you keep dying, child, always you
and the years keep slipping away.

Under the thinning leaves
and branches, you

with the red rose
taste of bitter death.

Not one dying throb of it
is spared you.

Endlessly, I cry . . . . .
in the night, for you my dear, in my heart,

and still that lullaby in my throat,
those sobbing notes I sang you while you died.

These eyes of mine turn no more
to the world;

the green leaves make them sorry.
— But the eternal lives inside me.

Love of you is the image of God
permitted me in this world.

I saw the angels crying too,
in the wind where the wet snow fell.

They hovered . . . .
in a heavenly draft.

Wenn der Mond in Blüte steht
Gleicht er deinem Leben, mein Kind.

Und ich mag nicht hinsehen
Wie der lichtspendende Falter sorglos dahinschwebt.

Nie ahnte ich den Tod
— Spüren um dich, mein Kind —

Und ich liebe des Zimmers Wände,
Die ich bemale mit deinem Knabenantlitz.

Die Sterne, die in diesem Monat
So viele sprühend ins Leben fallen,
Tropfen schwer auf mein Herz.

1943

The moon in its full flower
calls to mind my child in life.

And now I cannot bear to see
the butterfly float in a sorrowless light.

I never thought how death
kept closing on you, my sweet child.

I love the walls of your room,
where I paint your face in boyhood.

The usual stars that fall
this time of year are burning
this time into my heart.

Die Verscheuchte

Es ist der Tag im Nebel völlig eingehüllt,
Entseelt begegnen alle Welten sich —
Kaum hingezeichnet wie auf einem Schattenbild.

Wie lange war kein Herz zu meinem mild . . .
Die Welt erkaltete, der Mensch verblich.
— Komm bete mit mir — denn Gott tröstet mich.

Wo weilt der Odem, der aus meinem Leben wich?
Ich streife heimatlos zusammen mit dem Wild
Durch bleiche Zeiten träumend — ja ich liebte dich . . . . .

Wo soll ich hin, wenn kalt der Nordsturm brüllt?
Die scheuen Tiere aus der Landschaft wagen sich
Und ich vor deine Tür, ein Bündel Wegerich.

Bald haben Tränen alle Himmel weggespült,
An deren Kelchen Dichter ihren Durst gestillt —
Auch du und ich.

1943

The One They Frightened Away

The whole day wrapped in fog,
where worlds in limbo meet —
mere shadow puppets of themselves.

How long, my heart, since any kindness . . .
since this world grew cold, and people faded.
Come, the two of us, let's pray. God comforts me.

Where is the living breath once mine?
I pass among the drifting herds of deer
as faintly as a dream — yes, I did love you . . . . .

Where shall I go when the north wind roars
with ice? Shy creatures of the wild make way,
and at your door my flower, soft as mullein.

Soon my tears will wash away the very stars
from heaven. At this cup the poet's thirst
took ease — as did you, and I.

Herbst

Ich pflücke mir am Weg das letzte Tausendschön . . . . .
Es kam ein Engel mir mein Totenkleid zu nähen —
Denn ich muß andere Welten weiter tragen.

Das ewige Leben *dem*, der viel von Liebe weiß zu sagen.
Ein Mensch der Liebe kann nur auferstehen!
Haß schachtelt ein! wie hoch die Fackel auch mag schlagen.

Ich will dir viel viel Liebe sagen —
Wenn auch schon kühle Winde wehen,
In Wirbeln sich um Bäume drehen,
Um Herzen, die in ihren Wiegen lagen.

Mir ist auf Erden weh geschehen. . . . .
Der Mond gibt Antwort dir auf deine Fragen.
Er sah verhängt mich auch an Tagen,
Die zaghaft ich beging auf Zehen.

1943

Fall

The one last daisy by the path I pick for me . . . . .
An angel came to stitch my burial clothes —
I must be next, it seems, in another world.

Eternal life to those who speak much love.
Those born in love can only rise again!
Hate shuts the pit! high though the flare may burn.

And much I wish to speak to you, much love —
though cold winds reel by now
around the trees, around the hearts
that in their cradles lay.

Trouble was my portion in the world. . . . .
The moon gives answer to your questionings,
the moon who saw me on those cloudy days
when I went tiptoe still, and faint of heart.

Ein Liebeslied

Komm zu mir in der Nacht — wir schlafen engverschlungen.
Müde bin ich sehr, vom Wachen einsam.
Ein fremder Vogel hat in dunkler Frühe schon gesungen,
Als noch mein Traum mit sich und mir gerungen.

Es öffnen Blumen sich vor allen Quellen
Und färben sich mit deiner Augen Immortellen . . . . .

Komm zu mir in der Nacht auf Siebensternenschuhen
Und Liebe eingehüllt spät in mein Zelt.
Es steigen Monde aus verstaubten Himmelstruhen.

Wir wollen wie zwei seltene Tiere liebesruhen
Im hohen Rohre hinter dieser Welt.

1943